essentials

Hiring People

The things that really matter about

Hiring People

Steve Kneeland

Viva Books

New Delhi | Mumbai | Chennai | Kolkata | Bangalore | Hyderabad | Kochi

First Indian Edition 2000
Reprinted 2005, 2007

VIVA BOOKS PRIVATE LIMITED

- 4737/23 Ansari Road, Daryaganj, New Delhi 110 002
E-mail: vivadelhi@vivagroupindia.net, Tel. 42242200
- Plot No. 76, Service Industries, Shirvane, Sector 1, Nerul, Navi Mumbai 400 706
E-mail: vivamumbai@vivagroupindia.net, Tel. 27721273, 27721274
- Jamals Fazal Chambers, 26 Greams Road, Chennai 600 006
E-mail: vivachennai@vivagroupindia.net, Tel. 28290304, 28294241
- B-103, Jindal Towers, 21/1A/3 Darga Road, Kolkata 700 017
E-mail: vivakolkata@vivagroupindia.net, Tel. 22836381, 22816713
- 7, Sovereign Park Apartments, 56-58, K. R. Road, Basavanagudi, Bangalore 560 004
E-mail: vivabangalore@vivagroupindia.net, Tel. 26607409, 26607410
- 101-102 Mughal Marc Apartments, 3-4-637 to 641, Narayanguda, Hyderabad 500 029
E-mail: vivahyderabad@vivagroupindia.net, Tel. 27564481, 27564482
- Bee Vee Towers, First Floor, SRM Road, Kaloor, Kochi 682 018, Kerala
E-mail: vivakochi@vivagroupindia.net

Published by arrangement with

How to Books Limited
3 Newtec Place
Magdalen Road
Oxford OX4 1RE
UK

ESSENTIALS is an imprint of How to Books.

ISBN 81-7649-139-X

Published by Vinod Vasishtha for Viva Books Private Limited, 4737/23, Ansari Road, New Delhi 110 002. Printed and bound by Print Perfect, New Delhi - 110 064.

Contents

Preface

This book is written to achieve one specific goal – to hire people who will be outstanding performers. The amount of time and money invested in bringing a new person up to speed is considerable. And the difference between recruiting an average performer versus an outstanding performer, in terms of actual results achieved, is substantial. There's an awful lot at stake. Our goal in this book is to give the reader a clear strategy for the interview process, a set of practical tools to use, and a coherent framework within which to assess what various candidates have to offer.

Steven Kneeland

1 Pinning Down What's Needed

When you hire someone you need to know whether their past actions are what's needed for a successful performance in this job.

4

things that really matter

1. STARTING WITH THE JOB DESCRIPTION
2. FOCUSING ON BEHAVIOUR
3. LOOKING AT WHAT PEOPLE ACTUALLY DO
4. AVOIDING THE PITFALLS

As a manager you have to ask yourself what are the key things you want a person to possess that will generate a successful performance in the vacancy you want to fill. You must also make sure that by the time you are ready to recruit you have a clear picture of what the job requires.

This has to be your starting point and must be covered properly, engaging all the relevant personnel who are involved with the job. Don't leave anything to chance. If you want the successful candidate to be outstanding, and that should always be your goal, you must determine exactly what you want them to do.

Start by examining precisely what your top performers did for you before and look to re-create that in your winning candidate.

Identify the key things your top people do in their successful performances and look for them when you interview and evaluate a candidate for the job.

IS THIS YOU?

• *I've got to replace one of my team leaders and she's such a multi-skilled individual I don't know where to start.* • *I need to hire someone with real communication skills who can fit into the marketing team.* • *We're moving to a new product line and I need to appoint someone who has the experience to make the move as seamless as possible.* • *I've got to replace one of my regional sales managers who was such a top performer we left him to his own devices. Now I'm not sure what to look for in his replacement.*

STARTING WITH THE JOB DESCRIPTION

The job description must outline the key duties and responsibilities involved in the job as well as the reporting relationships and the number of people supervised. It should also include the goals that have to be achieved and the performance standards that must be satisfied.

You need to identify what the job requires in the way of **knowledge**, **skills** and job related qualities.

- **Knowledge factors** are required in most jobs and are usually known as technical knowledge or expertise. This can be a specific knowledge in standard costing systems or a broader knowledge such as a good grasp of business fundamentals or basic understanding of how to manage people. When people fail through lack of knowledge it is generally in the broader area.
- **Skills factors**, like knowledge, aren't directly observable but you can see them being used or, perhaps more to the point, not being used. Examine each of the areas of responsibility on the job description and you will see what skills are going to be needed. There are the

specific skills like those of project management, systems analysis or a sound mechanical understanding that are central to many jobs. There are also the broader aspects such as those of planning, analysis, conceptual awareness, persuasion, leadership and presentational skills. When people fail through lack of skills it is generally in the latter, broader area.

Once you have identified what the job requires in the way of knowledge, skills and job-related qualities you will know what you should be seeking from the candidate in the interview.

2 FOCUSING ON BEHAVIOUR

Your focus should be on hiring people who will produce outstanding performances. That means you need to identify the candidate's behaviour in previous jobs.

To do this you need to:

- observe the candidate's past performance and
- on the basis of that past performance, project the candidate's future performance in the job you're offering.

You can do this by targeting, or digging for, the specific behaviour that would have been central to the candidate's previous outstanding performances during the interview.

You must plan the interview process accordingly by ensuring you have the personnel and expertise available at the interview to conduct searching inquiries and that they are fully prepared for the task ahead.

By taking a behavioural approach to the interview you come as close as you can to actually watching the candidate in action.

Regard the knowledge and skills factors as minimum

standards for recruitment and use them for selecting those candidates you wish to interview for the job. What you should be searching for is that quintessential something that produces **outstanding** performance.

You know that the job description calls for the ideal candidate to possess good communication skills, be a team player and be ambitious but you must be clear in knowing exactly what that means. You need to define precisely what behaviour you will be looking for in the candidate to achieve these qualities.

3 LOOKING AT WHAT PEOPLE ACTUALLY DO

To describe behaviour you need to identify the behavioural patterns that are needed in the job. The best way to do this is to look at the behaviour of people already in that job.

You should ask two important questions:

- What specific behaviours do you see in your people that account for them producing good results? What specific behaviours do you see that you wish everyone would display?
- What specific behaviours do you see in your people that seem to impede successful performance?

When you identify those bits and pieces of behaviour marking the difference between outstanding and average performance in a job you can sort them into meaningful patterns and give them a name.

For example. Your top people in this job might:

- Take some time at the outset of the day to sort out their priorities.
- Spend at least half an hour preparing for an important meeting.

- Go into a meeting with a clearly understood and written agenda.
- Have anticipated key questions they would have to deal with and have prepared well thought through answers to them.
- Know what they want to come away from a meeting with. They know what outcomes they want to achieve.

You can see there's a pattern here. Your top people obviously exhibit a good behaviour of forward planning so call it just that. You now know that **forward planning** is a behaviour central to this job and is something you want to see in the winning candidate.

It's worth remembering that, although one of your team has put together a list of behavioural or performance characteristics that are important to this job, you should take this information with a pinch of salt. Treat the list only as a useful starting point and get out there to see what specific behaviours are at work for yourself.

For example. Does communication skills mean that someone is:

- Good at making small talk and getting people to relax without getting too familiar or overdoing things?
- Good at making the point first with an overview, then provides the details before going back to the overview?
- Good because they made the finance manager smile the other day?
- Good at being bubbly with the sales people yet analytical and businesslike with the technical people?

It's important that you are clear in your own mind exactly what types of behaviour are required for the vacancy you want to fill. If communication skills seem to be the agreed requirement, make sure everyone knows what behaviour is meant by it and how it manifests itself within the job.

④ AVOIDING THE PITFALLS

There is a potential problem if you apply too literally the analysis of what makes your successful people succeed and then look for those characteristics in your winning candidate.

The pitfalls are:

- The behavioural pattern is rarely a clear-cut one.
- People can compensate for their shortcomings.
- A good quality can be carried too far.
- What you think is needed can change.
- Technical specifications can be over emphasised.

The behavioural pattern is rarely a clear-cut one. You will generally find certain levels of skills in most jobs. Without basic keyboard skills, for example, a candidate for a job as an order entry clerk would not be hired.

Once you go beyond the obvious, however, it is rarely possible to pin down exactly what any given job requires for successful performance. In the case of most jobs the top performers tend to be rather unique in how they achieve their results. They may be alike in certain respects but not to the point where you could say there is a single **definitive** behaviour that defines successful performance.

People can compensate for their shortcomings. Even if you know for sure that a certain skill is needed for success in the job you should still exercise caution. For example, a person may be quite average when it comes to being a self-starter but may achieve outstanding results through good planning and faultless organisation when working with clearly defined goals and well established guidelines.

A good quality can be carried too far. You must be aware of this as it's a very subtle danger. A desirable characteristic – whether it be assertiveness or a concern for detail – can have undesirable consequences if taken to extremes.

For example, in searching for the candidate with assertiveness you may inadvertently hire the one who irritates people with their aggressiveness and inability to listen.

What you think is needed can change. Don't make the mistake of hiring someone to solve yesterday's problems rather than hiring the one needed to take advantage of tomorrow's opportunities.

The person you hire this year will have to be better than most of the ones you hired three years ago for a variety of reasons. You were looking for a different type of person then. In the same way, the ingredients needed to produce outstanding performances will not be the same now as it was then.

Technical specifications can be over emphasised. People usually succeed or fail in a job for reasons which have more to do with operating style and inter-personal skills than with technical skills or knowledge.

By all means use technical qualifications and specific experience as a method of screening in the selection process but don't use it as reason for hiring or not hiring.

There is the added danger too, that, if you draw up lists of specific qualities and credentials that you feel the winning candidate must have, you spend too much time worrying about the sort of person you're looking for rather than the sort of person who's looking at you. Use your experience to get a *feel* for the candidate and how they would perform in the job. Don't worry about **evaluating** the candidate's predicted performance during the interview.

Focus all your attention on **predicting** it.

Try imagining the candidate actually doing the job. Focus on aspects of the job where specific behaviours are required without being too strict about it. If communication skills are required, ask the candidate to relate a particularly difficult achievement they claim to have accomplished.

MAKING WHAT MATTERS WORK FOR YOU

- ✓ Make sure your job description identifies the knowledge and skills relevant to the job.
- ✓ Focus on the candidate's behaviour so that you can bring past performance to bear on the future.
- ✓ Identify what behaviours your top people are doing now to produce outstanding performance and look for it in your winning candidates.
- ✓ Remember to exercise caution when applying the analysis of what makes your successful people outstanding performers. Don't apply it too literally as things always change.

2 Cracking the CV

Studying the CV is an integral part of the selection process and it serves a number of important purposes.

6 things that really matter

1. IDENTIFYING THE WINNING CANDIDATE'S PROFILE
2. ESTABLISHING THE CANDIDATE'S BACKGROUND
3. ASSESSING THE CANDIDATE'S WORK EXPERIENCE
4. STUDYING THE EDUCATIONAL BACKGROUND
5. IDENTIFYING CAREER PROGRESS
6. SORTING THE CVs

The CV gives you a summary of the candidate's work experience with dates, company names, job titles, and details of what was involved in each position. It will also indicate salary, special achievements and the reasons for leaving each previous employer.

Use it as an integral part of the recruitment process. If you had to use the interview to obtain this information there would be little time left for the crucial task of exploring how the candidate actually performs.

The CV enables you to whittle the list of candidates down to a manageable size by matching the previous behavioural patterns of the candidate to the qualities you know are important for the vacancy you want to fill.

It also enables you to prepare your targeting strategies for the interview. These will be important when picking the candidate who will provide you with outstanding performance.

IS THIS YOU?

• *I've got to draw up a longlist of candidates for the IT post and I don't have enough time to read each CV word for word.* • *I need a surefire method of sorting the possibles from the probables in this pile of CVs.* • *How will I know whether I'm removing the right candidates from the longlist?* • *How will I know if I'm placing the strongest candidates on the shortlist?*

IDENTIFYING THE WINNING CANDIDATE'S PROFILE

You have to make the assumption that outstanding performers possess certain qualities regardless of their specific qualities or skills. Think of these in terms of qualities that you would consider to be essential in the winning candidate's profile. They are:

- **Goal orientation.** You need to know that the candidate has developed the habit of setting specific goals and works steadily towards their achievement.
- **Organisation.** Does the candidate pursue their goals in an intelligent, disciplined and **effective** manner? Planning ahead, thinking about what has to be done, focusing on the things that count.
- **Initiative.** Is the candidate the sort of person who makes things happen? Who isn't prepared to let others waste valuable time by waiting for someone else to make decisions for them.
- **Intelligence.** You need to know that the candidate thinks on their feet, meeting the intellectual requirements of both this job and the one after that as well.

The CV is the first step in a series of progressively demanding hurdles over which the candidate must pass in order to land the job.

- **Relationship building.** You need to know if the candidate is a good team player and is able to bridge the gap that so often separates departments and functions. That the person will be an asset to have around.
- **Communication skills.** Can the candidate communicate ideas and concepts? Do they recognise that communication happens in the minds and hearts of the audience and not in the words of the speaker.
- **Leadership.** Is the candidate confident and assertive enough to move the agenda along at the appropriate pace, to impose deadlines and standards without necessarily having the authority to do so and will they have the strength to defend an idea or a proposal?
- **Enthusiasm.** You need to know that the candidate is a positive, upbeat, enthusiastic type of person who gets keenly involved in their work and whose manner **communicates** that enthusiasm to those around them. Is it a vibrant, visible quality that others can see and be affected by?
- **Drive.** Is the candidate the sort of person who doesn't settle for the average? Are they determined to achieve outstanding results?
- **Resilience.** You need to know whether the candidate can rebound quickly after a setback. Can they deal with the obstacles, problems and frustrations that often accompany poor results. Is their self-confidence too fragile?
- **Self-development**. Does the candidate practise continuous learning? Do they work on their **effectiveness** and search for ways to put their talents to optimal use?

- **Stayability.** You need to know whether the candidate intends to stay with you to repay the investment you will make in terms of training and development. Performers can't be outstanding if they leave after 12 months in the job.

2 ESTABLISHING THE CANDIDATE'S BACKGROUND

Use the CV to establish the candidate's general details:

- name
- address
- telephone number
- education
- job-related training
- work experience with dates, company names and job details
- professional or industrial involvement
- hobbies and recreational pursuits.

Force yourself to generate as many hypotheses about the candidate as you can from the background given in their CV. Decide what areas of information you need to explore or probe more specifically during the interview.

Don't make the mistake of passing judgement on a candidate at this stage. All you're doing here is drawing up hypotheses, not conclusions.

Don't just read the CV. Digest it. Take notes.

3 ASSESSING THE CANDIDATE'S WORK EXPERIENCE

It is important that you identify whether the candidate has the appropriate work experience to do the job for which they are being considered.

To do this you need to look at what specific things the candidate was **responsible** for in each position. Look at what segment of the company they worked in, who they reported to and what projects they were involved with.

Look for **results**. Make sure you know what the candidate achieved and how significant those achievements were for the company, product or project they were dealing with.

Look for evidence that the candidate has already successfully done the **type of work** you want them to do for you.

An outstanding candidate will want to tell you the results of everything they have accomplished.

If you're hiring someone for a sales position, for example, give them one point for any sales experience, another for having worked in your industry and another for having handled a competitive or related product line. Give them a point for having called upon the same type of customer your people are calling upon.

④ STUDYING THE EDUCATIONAL BACKGROUND

Ideally you need to look for evidence of education beyond the secondary school level. Then check exactly what **type** of education the candidate has followed. A good balance is some experience in the sciences, to suggest an affinity for technical subject matter, and some in history or literature to reflect a well-rounded individual.

Be wary of too much education or examples of advanced areas of study that are completely unrelated to anything the candidate has done in the past or plans to use in the future.

Look carefully, too, at the **subjects** taken. See if the

courses were in the hard, tangible disciplines or in the more abstract, theoretical ones. This shouldn't preclude a candidate from your consideration for the job but it can give you an insight into their **motivational attributes** and about their affinity for tangible problem-solving as opposed to theoreticising about what should and can be done.

4 IDENTIFYING CAREER PROGRESS

You can determine a lot about your candidate's **suitability** for the job by looking at their past behaviour.

The person who has progressed rapidly will probably expect to continue in the same way. You must recognise that this can be a positive sign of motivation, drive and ability but it can also be an indicator of potential frustration.

Companies don't usually let an outstanding performer linger too long in one job or at the same organisational level.

Make sure you look for **career progress**. Don't mistake this for just career movement. An indicator of progress is where the education element dovetails into the work history and where the candidate took on increasingly challenging assignments.

If a candidate has had several jobs without making significant progress it could reflect a lack of drive and ambition where they avoided responsibility or higher levels of pressure.

Similarly, check if a candidate has spent more than five years in the same job. It doesn't always mean there is a problem but it is worth targeting in the interview.

Don't be too quick to judge at this stage and the following points will be helpful in drawing up your hypotheses:

- **Looking for career stability.** Beware of the candidate who has changed jobs frequently, particularly if the changes have not been accompanied by visible career advancement. Check, though, that the person hasn't been the unwitting victim of redundancies.
- **Spotting portable assets.** You must look for those tangible skills, experiences, training, insights and product knowledge the candidate will bring to the job. These are portable assets and the more there are, the less adjustment will be needed and the more immediate will be the candidate's contribution.
- **Communication skills.** The CV is your first glimpse of the candidate's communication skills. It should be well organised and convey its meaning simply and succinctly. As a general rule, don't accept sloppy composition or handwriting, errors – either scratched out or left in, uneven margins, mistakes in grammar or spelling, the use of flowery language and excessively ornate or expensive paper. Remember that mistakes here could well be repeated in the work the candidate does for you in the job.
- **Indications of attitude.** You will find that many candidates are inadvertently revealing underlying attitudes in the information they give in their CV. If they state that they left a job through a disagreement over policy it could indicate an inability to adapt to the corporate environment. However you interpret this it's worth remembering that a candidate is showing a certain degree of naivety merely by including it on their CV.
- **Indications of initiative.** Don't miss little gems that reflect initiative. If a candidate states that they worked evenings in order to get through college regard it as an

indication that they are self-reliant and resourceful. Admirable qualities that will come to the fore in producing outstanding performance.

Good candidates usually present their achievements and let them speak for themselves.

- **Looking at the covering letter.** The candidate should include a covering letter unless you specifically state otherwise. Not to do so reflects a basic lack of courtesy. It should address the specific situation and be applied to your specific needs for the job. Think of it as a sales letter with you being the prospective customer and the candidate being the product. In general, the best type of covering letter avoids self-evaluations. The CV should provide all that is required and the letter should present a mature, down-to-earth attempt at encouraging you to look at the writer's application for the job in more detail.
- **The candidate's follow-up.** You should be aware of what the candidate does after sending their CV for your attention. If they have made a follow-up call to check it has arrived safely then give them some extra marks – as long as it was done professionally and maturely. Make sure you're informed if the candidate makes a nuisance of themself and mark them down accordingly. It's worth remembering that the behaviour you see here is what your customers and colleagues will be seeing if you hire this person.

5 SORTING THE CVs

You can use the CV as the first step in the recruitment process to screen out those candidates who aren't what you're looking for at this time and look more deeply at those you're interested in. **Screening** someone out is a very important decision and must be made on the basis of something obvious and tangible.

You can do it in one of two ways:

- **Sorting the CVs into two piles.** Place those that are clearly suitable and warrant further interest into one pile and those that are obviously unsuitable into another. Applicants that are suitable can be earmarked for interviews. Those in the unsuitable pile can now be informed of your decision not to proceed with them any further. The two-pile strategy is suitable when there is a relatively small number of applicants for the job.
- **Sorting the CVs into three piles.** This is the strategy to use when you have a larger number of applicants to deal with. As before, create one pile immediately for those who are obviously unsuitable or unqualified. Generate a second pile for those who really stimulate your interest and keep a third for those you're not absolutely sure about but are reluctant to eliminate completely at this stage. By doing this, you are seeking a judicious balance between the need to minimise interviewing time and the need to do enough interviewing to ensure you hire the best candidate. Don't be too judgemental at this stage. Judging candidates on paper is difficult and if you're going to err at all it's better to err by interviewing too many candidates than by losing potentially outstanding performers through your CV screening process.

Trust your instincts with the CV. Assume that what you see is representative of what customers and colleagues would see if this person were hired.

MAKING WHAT MATTERS WORK FOR YOU

- ✓ Assume that outstanding performers possess certain qualities which make up the winning candidate's profile.
- ✓ Generate hypotheses from the candidate's general background and decide what you need to explore further during the interview.
- ✓ Look for evidence that the candidate's work experience is appropriate for the job for which they are being considered.
- ✓ Go for a good balanced educational background that will give you a well-rounded individual.
- ✓ Look for career progress where education, training, drive, ambition and portable assets combine to give you a potentially outstanding performer.
- ✓ Sort the CVs into two or three piles depending upon the number of applications you have.

3 Planning for the Interview

A lot of information has to be gathered in a limited period of time and the interview will be the basis for some critical decisions.

4 things that really matter

1. PREPARING FOR THE INTERVIEW
2. PREPARING A SIMPLE PLAN
3. THE TOOLS YOU'LL BE USING
4. EXAMINING THE FIVE INTERVIEW AREAS

There are two things taking place in every interview. There's the **content** of the interview, where you and the candidate spend time talking about a range of topics, either spontaneously or pre-scripted, and you get to know the candidate as best as you can.

There's also the **mental** side of the interview, where you're drawing up and testing out hypotheses about the sort of person the candidate is, and whether they have the make-up you're looking for in an outstanding performer.

Don't make the mistake of thinking that the discursive aspect of the interview comprises small talk. No time should be wasted and if small talk helps to break the ice make it sound **real** rather than **feigned**.

Planning for the interview calls for the same amount of forethought and preparation that you would apply to an important sales presentation or a management meeting.

IS THIS YOU?

• I'm interviewing a shortlist of high calibre candidates this week and I've got little time to prepare myself for the interview. How can I make sure I hire the outstanding performer? • I asked my boss for advice in preparing for the interviews but she just told me to use my initiative and judgement. • I've only interviewed candidates for minor positions before. This is my first big one and I'm not sure exactly how to prepare for it. • I've gathered together all the background information about the job, now I need to organise my interview process so that I can fit that and the information I shall learn about the candidates into the formula that will help me identify the person I should hire.

PREPARING FOR THE INTERVIEW

There are three important things you have to do in preparation:

- **Ensure your purpose is clear.** Don't wander aimlessly from one topic to another during the interview because your objectives have been only vaguely established. If you're using a two interview strategy you should use the first to see whether the candidate has the basic personal qualities you desire before deciding whether or not to proceed to a second interview. If you're using a single interview strategy you'll have to be **brisk** in acquiring an impression of the candidate's personal qualities so that you can immediately probe more deeply before making a decision.

Decide beforehand exactly what it is you wish to accomplish during the interview.

- **Review the available information.** Familiarise yourself with the candidate's CV well before they arrive for interview. If the candidate has been subject to some form of testing earlier in the procedure, **analyse** the results and see how they tie in with the information you've gathered about them.

- **Plan the main topics you want to cover in the interview.** Then determine how much time you should devote to each one. Make a note of specific questions you want to ask from the background information you've already gathered. Make the plan as detailed as possible but recognise the need for **flexibility** in its execution.

2 PREPARING A SIMPLE PLAN

A plan does two important things:

- **It keeps you in control of things.** There's less rambling, fewer false starts, and fewer unproductive sidetracks. You're never left wondering what you should talk about next.
- **It helps you cover what needs to be covered.** It ensures that all topic areas are explored systematically, with less danger of you giving one area too much emphasis at the expense of others and a reduced chance of your impressions being based upon a limited sampling of the candidate's experience.

Bear in mind that you have a lot to squeeze into a short interview period but, because you'll have so much ground to cover, you are compelled to move things along smartly.

The following plan will help:

- Start with a bit of **small talk**, not too much, to help the candidate relax.

- Talk about the basic purpose of the interview and how you'll do it. Make sure the basic **groundrules** are clear.
- Begin discussion of the candidate's **background**. You can start with their formal education if you wish.
- Move into a chronological review of the candidate's **work history** ending with their current or most recent position.
- Talk about their **career goals and aspirations**. Where would they like to be in five years time?
- Talk specifically about why the job is **attractive** to them, how it fits into their **career** plans and how it will help them get where they want to go.
- Finally, put work-related issues aside and talk about family, social life and hobbies. Talk about the **personal side** of things.

Impress upon the candidate that the interview will be exploratory, with questions covering a wide range of topics and that they must feel free to pose questions of their own at any stage in the proceedings. They must know that it's a meeting of two intelligent and enquiring minds rather than a one-sided investigation of them as an individual.

3 THE TOOLS YOU'LL BE USING

Once you've settled the candidate into a suitably relaxed and focused frame of mind you should use three main tools to make the interview as successful as you can.

The LEAD-IN takes the form of an open-ended question that you use to move into each major stage of the interview or to introduce a new subject within a stage. There are two rules to keep in mind:

- First, keep the lead-in **open ended**. Don't move into a new area by asking a specific, or closed, question. Start by – 'You've been with the Post Office for four years ... tell me what you've been doing?'
- Second, after asking the lead-in question **let the candidate talk** without interruption.

You must create the opportunity of seeing the candidate **at work** whenever possible and you do that by posing an open-ended question that effectively requires them to resolve a problem. Then you take careful note of how they handled it:

- Did the candidate get **flustered** and ask for more direction? Was it handled smoothly and did the candidate display lots of **poise**?
- Did the candidate take too long to stop and think, obviously planning their overall approach, before getting started? Be careful here because a short time of reflection is often better than getting immediate and rehearsed answers. Use your **judgement** if you think the candidate has taken more time than you'd expect, or displays certain body language, over a question you think should have been handled better.
- Did the candidate ramble on to the point where you were forced to move in? Be wary of someone who gets bogged down in excessive detail.

The second tool you'll be using is **The PROBE**. It generally starts with **what, who, where, why** or **how** and conveys a very simple message of *tell me more*.

Probes don't have to be questions. They can be expressed in the form of a mild directive like 'Tell me a little more about why you left ... ?'

Show that you're really **interested** in what the candidate has to say, that you're eager to find out exactly what happened.

Your probe can also take the form of a **reflective statement** that asks the candidate to confirm that you've drawn the right conclusion like

- 'So you felt the meeting would be a waste of time if the CEO wasn't there. . . ?'

Sometimes a **gesture** will do. Raise an eyebrow, cock your head to one side, and widen your eyes. Gestures of this sort tell the candidate you're reacting to something they've said and you want to hear more.

The FOLLOW-UP is the third tool you'll be using. It's a question you use to get at specific things the candidate didn't talk about spontaneously in response to your initial lead-in.

Here are some examples:

- 'If you could go back and do your college years again, is there anything you'd change or do differently?'
- 'Looking back on it now, how do you feel about the way your career has unfolded? Is it the "real" you?'

Note that your follow-up questions are a bit more **specific** than the open ended lead-in but they're not too much so. Like the lead-in, they're an invitation to talk but within narrower boundaries.

You should have a set of follow-up questions for each stage of the interview that will **stimulate** discussion and elicit useful information. Get used to asking them routinely at every interview. Make sure they sound like you and that you can present them in a conversational fashion. If you can, get so accustomed to using them that you are able to adapt them to suit the specific type of candidate you're dealing with.

Even when the questions you're asking are open-ended avoid asking too many. The interview should be more than just a question and answer session.

Too heavy a reliance on the question as a means of stimulating conversation can result in the following problems:

- **The candidate may become defensive.** Remember that every time you ask a question the candidate presumes the subject matter must be important and will tread carefully when formulating a reply. This then ceases to be a conversation.
- **Less information will be forthcoming.** By asking too many questions you are, in effect, telling the candidate that if you want to know something, you'll ask. This obviously impedes the flow of genuine conversation and, by the same token, also impedes the amount of information you wish to acquire from the candidate.
- **It places a burden upon you as the interviewer.** If you allow the interview to descend into a question and answer session it falls upon you to keep things going by formulating questions all the time. As a consequence, you have little time to either hear, or think about, what the candidate is actually saying.

④ EXAMINING THE FIVE INTERVIEW AREAS

The content of the interview is divided into five main areas whilst your assessment of what the candidate has to offer is spread across the 12 factors or qualities making up the winning candidate's profile covered earlier.

The five main areas are:

- Identifying the educational background.
- Recognising the work history.
- Checking for career goals and aspirations.
- Why this specific opportunity?
- Checking out the candidate's personal life and hobbies.

Identifying the educational background

You'll already have a sketchy outline from the CV but use a **lead-in** like

- 'I see you did some under-graduate work at Leeds. I was there too. What did you think of it?'

This gives the candidate an idea that you want to talk about education before you dig deeper with a **probe** to get at the details and then **follow-ups** to confirm the specific aspects you're looking for.

The following list will help you apply those relevant parts of the winning candidate's profile to this area:

- **Goal orientation.** Give higher marks to the candidate whose education was consciously chosen to fit into a long-term career plan that was realistic at the time and which has been successfully executed.
- **Organisation.** Look for signs that the candidate tackled their educational goals in a **specific**, **systematic** and **disciplined** manner.
- **Intelligence.** You can find out a lot about someone by the content of their education. The level of difficulty of their courses. The number of extra courses they undertook. The results they achieved in their modular tests.

- **Relationship building.** Give high marks to the candidate who made friendships that have endured to the present.
- **Drive.** Look for signs that the candidate has **commitment**, is able to make tough choices and has made sacrifices to achieve this far. If a person has worked to support themselves financially through college it tells you a lot about their personality and character.
- **Stayability.** You need to determine whether the candidate has a basic **affinity** for the work you're offering.

Recognising the work history

In most cases this will be the most important part of the interview. You can explore this by either dealing with it in reverse order, starting with what the candidate is doing now and working backwards, or reviewing it in chronological order, normally starting from when they left school.

You'll need the candidate's CV available so you can probe for more detail as they talk and you should keep the following questions in the back of your mind:

- **How and why** did the candidate take the job?
- **What** was the job all about?
- What **specific challenges** did they face?
- How well did they **perform**?
- **Why** did they leave?

The specific areas to be covered here are:

Goal orientation. You'll find that it's instructive to talk about how a candidate has tackled a major project. As they talk, probe for specifics by using the following:

- Did the candidate start by clarifying **goals and**

deadlines, thinking through the overall strategy, and putting together a step-by-step action plan?

- Did the candidate use a **critical path** approach with specific dates attached to each step?
- Was the candidate **realistic** in the estimates of how long things would take?
- Did the candidate make full use of all available **resources**?
- Did the candidate **involve** others when appropriate?
- Did the candidate talk to people who would be **affected** by the project or who were intended to be its beneficiaries?

It's always revealing to ask a candidate how they plan their day as it's often an unexpected question and you will not get a rehearsed answer. Look too, for evidence that the candidate can distinguish between what's urgent and what's important.

Effective performers don't just prioritise what's on their schedule. They schedule their priorities.

Initiative. You often have to dig for initiative using probe and follow-up questions. It can only be assessed by looking at what went through the candidate's mind when they were dealing with a specific problem. A simple thing like **re-scheduling** an important meeting at short notice with people from various departments can involve great difficulty and it requires initiative to achieve it successfully.

Intelligence. Find out about any **training** the candidate has received, or what knowledge they have about the product, or how quickly they've had to think on their feet. Was there a high level of **analysis** involved with the work? These are important areas that will tell you whether the candidate has the practical, above average intelligence needed to do the job properly.

Relationship-building. Look for signs that the candidate has played an **active** role in committees or has been involved in special industry groups or professional associations.

Leadership. Look for evidence of the candidate getting projects through committees and management groups where a bit of selling and arm twisting was required.

Self-development. Find out what the candidate has learned from a specific job. Ask them what they did to bring themselves up to speed. Look beyond the training that was built into their job and **probe** what they did of their own accord to enhance their performance potential.

Stayability. You have to pay special attention to the candidate's reaction to the various jobs they've had and the companies they've worked for. You should also look at why they turned down offers of employment in favour of another employer. Probe deeply here as you will be able to establish the working environment most suited to the candidate.

How well did the candidate perform? You can learn a lot about previous job behaviour by asking the candidate to assess their performance in specific situations. Successful people focus on their results to keep track of what they're doing.

There are a number of ways you can probe for this by asking:

- '**How** would you personally **evaluate** your performance in that job?'

- '**How** was your **performance** in that job evaluated by other people?'
- 'If you could go back and do that job again, are there things that you would do differently?'

Look also for tangible signs of above average achievement in the form of special awards, membership of the special achievers club or year end bonuses. You must press for details here as every employee might acquire membership of the achievers club!

Successful people focus on results and on contribution and they keep track of how well they're doing.

Why did the candidate leave? You get an indication of the candidate's behaviour by establishing their reasons for leaving a job. You often have to probe here rather than accepting the candidate's initial version of things.

Tread carefully here and don't always assume that a company wouldn't have let them go if they were good performers. By all means be a bit of a cynic but remember that good people have been made redundant for reasons other than being a poor performer.

Checking for career goals and aspirations

You must investigate what lies ahead in the candidate's career and there are two ways of doing this. First is to ask the candidate what they are looking for at this point in their career. Then talk more generally about the candidate's ideal job, the ideal boss and the ideal environment.

An experienced candidate will have prepared answers for this whilst a less experienced one will pause for thought. That doesn't necessarily mean that aspirations are less important to them.

Winning profile criteria here are:

Goal orientation. Outstanding performers tend to have specific goals, not general ones. Probe by asking:

- '**Where** do you see yourself going from here? Where would you like to be in five years time?'
- 'Are there other **options** that you're looking at, or have you made up your mind about things?'
- '**How** did you set those **goals**? Did you actually sit down, think them through and write them down?'

If you think the candidate is unclear in their responses you can use this as a good follow-up:

- 'Are there specific **yardsticks** or **benchmarks** that you would use to assess how your career is going? For some people, for example, it's how much money they're making, or being the number one performer on the team ... ?'

Don't press too hard. If you do there's a good chance that the candidate will invent some goals on the spot thus losing you the authenticity of the moment.

Stayability. You can get some indication of the candidate's stayability factor by asking the following questions:

- 'What are the things that are **important** to you in a job or in a company? Why?'
- 'What are some of the things you would wish to **avoid** in a job or company?'
- 'How would you **describe** the ideal boss? What sort of manager really brings out the best in you?'

The answers should give you an **insight** into whether you can satisfy the candidate's needs. Whether their goals are realistically achievable in the time frame available and, last but not least, whether the candidate and the job are actually compatible.

Why this specific opportunity?

You can discover some interesting aspects of both the candidate and your company by seeking their opinions about the job. Start with a lead-in like:

- 'I'd like to talk about your **view** of this particular opportunity. To start the ball rolling, do you have any basic questions about the job?'

Give the candidate the **opportunity** to ask as many questions as they wish. Let them talk freely before you ask your probing questions.

The following aspects of the winners profile apply here:

Self-development. You know that if you hire the candidate they will find themself on a learning curve. It pays to establish whether they have done an assessment of their skills and experience and how it fits the demands of the role. The following probes will help you:

- 'If you join us, you'll be dealing with a whole new customer base. What sort of **adjustments** do you think might be needed on your part?'
- 'I'm concerned that you haven't dealt with this complex a product before. What thoughts do you have on that?'
- 'Is there anything special that you've done to **prepare** yourself for this new assignment?'

Stayability. You should note that what a candidate is looking for and what they need are not always the same thing. They might want the job badly and see it as the next logical step in their career but if they need a lot of direction or can't keep a number of ideas running at the same time you are ill advised to hire them.

This is a crucial area and you must be satisfied with your decision and these questions will help:

- 'From where you stand, what do you see as the **main challenges** or difficulties in this job?'
- 'I've talked about some of the challenges we're facing out in the field and some of the new directions we're taking ... How do you see yourself making a **contribution**?'
- 'What appeals to you in this job that you've not had in your previous situation?'

Checking out the candidate's personal life and hobbies. You can easily get distracted here so try to zero in on the things that tell you something meaningful about the candidate. Use the following aspects of the winner's profile.

Goal orientation. It's useful to see if the candidate has set goals for themself in regard to their hobbies or leisure pursuits. It shouldn't apply to all of them as they should be pursued for sheer pleasure but it's relevant for them to have set goals in something.

It might be that the candidate wanted to learn a foreign language. Did they set specific goals in terms of **target dates** for completion, or for the type of assessment at the end of the course?

One sign of a healthy, well-balanced person is, after all, that they know how to relax.

Organisation. Ask the candidate to talk about an activity they had to **plan** in some detail. You'll be looking for evidence of an overall **strategy** that they translated into a coherent action plan. Look also to see if their plan was based on an accurate estimate of how long the activity would take or how much it would cost.

Relationship-building. Look for evidence of **sociability** in the candidate.

- Do they **belong** to any clubs?
- Are they **active** in the community?
- Do they seem to watch too much television?

Drive. Find out if the candidate enjoys a **competitive** edge to their hobbies. You should also establish whether they do something for a couple of months before getting bored with it or is it a lifetime pursuit. This can tell you a lot about their character.

You should be wary of someone who takes their hobby too seriously. Establish exactly what they do for a bit of fun and relax after the rigours of a hard week.

Stayability. This can be important for you because you should ask whether this person is right for you and your company. Ask it with some trepidation, as you must not allow your personal bias to come to the fore.

Outstanding performers, most often, are people who work hard and play hard.

Balanced lifestyle. If you look at your outstanding performers you'll see they attach importance to leisure time and don't waste it. Look for that in your candidate's background.

- Do they set **personal goals** of leisure time with their families?

- Do they **plan** their activities in advance?
- Do they engage in exercise?

Perhaps most important of all. Do they consciously acknowledge the importance of being fit and healthy insofar as being a productive, on-the job performer is concerned?

MAKING WHAT MATTERS WORK FOR YOU

✓ In preparing for the interview you must ensure your purpose is clear, review all the available information and plan exactly what you wish to cover.

✓ Prepare a plan that keeps you in control of things and helps you cover the important things.

✓ Use the important interview tools of the **lead-in, probe** and **follow-up** questions.

✓ Plan your interview around the five main areas of education, work history, career goals, this specific job and the candidate's personal life and hobbies.

4 Examining Strengths and Weaknesses

The traditional question of strengths and weaknesses may need to be raised explicitly.

6 things that really matter

1. STARTING WITH STRENGTHS
2. BEING PREPARED TO PROBE
3. LOOKING AT WEAKNESSES
4. USING A ONE-TWO COMBINATION
5. SELF-DEVELOPMENT
6. USING A QUESTIONNAIRE

Through your discussions with the candidate of their work history, and to a lesser extent their education and career goals, you may already be able to draw up a very accurate view of their strengths and weaknesses. It could be a mistake if you didn't devote a specific chunk of the interview to exploring this area as the impression you have might be inaccurate.

Most candidates will expect questions on this theme and will have prepared some answers that they will carefully drop into conversation across the whole interview process. You have to decide whether they're a candid self-appraisal or something straight out of a *How-to-Win-the-Interview* book they've just read.

Even if you think you're experienced enough to decipher these messages accurately you are still well advised to cover all eventualities by giving strengths and weaknesses time for a few questions.

IS THIS YOU?

• I think I've managed to identify the candidate's strengths and weaknesses but I don't think I'll leave it to chance. • We're looking for someone with specific strengths and experience to fill this job and I need to make sure I get it right first time. • How can I make sure the candidate is giving us an accurate picture of their strengths and weaknesses?

1 STARTING WITH STRENGTHS

Some candidates find this **threatening** so you move into the subject in a natural way from the preceding discussion without attaching a strengths or weaknesses label to the topic. It's best if you can talk about strengths first by starting with something like:

- 'We've talked about some of the things you've **achieved** over the past five years, and you seem to have done very well for yourself. What are some of the **specific** things about you that you feel have accounted for the success you've had?'

You might find that the candidate has difficulty getting started and a follow-up like this will help:

- 'Here's the type of thing I mean. I have a daughter who's really inquisitive, to the point where it drives me crazy at times. But I know that's always going to be one of her strengths and I want to encourage it.'

2 BEING PREPARED TO PROBE

Find out why something, in the candidate's view, is a strength. You may need to use a combination of follow-up questions and probes to reach a satisfactory conclusion.

Here's an example:

- 'What would you say there is about you that has **accounted** for your career progress to date?'
- 'How exactly has that "accounted for your career progress" ...?'
- 'What would you say are your main strengths? Areas where you are distinctly above average?'
- 'This probably sounds like an odd question, but ... how do you know that? **How do you know you're above average in that area?**'

You might want to issue a **mild challenge** if you don't agree with the candidate's view of their own strengths and weaknesses.

- 'You've mentioned assertiveness as being one of your strengths. I'll be quite honest with you, it's one of the things I'm a bit concerned about ... '

Another powerful question to ask the candidate is **why** they think you should **hire them**. It places the ball firmly in their court and, now that they know you're looking specifically at their strengths and weaknesses, they will be very careful how they phrase their answer.

3 LOOKING AT WEAKNESSES

Again, when you move on to weaknesses, do so in a **conversational** way that flows easily. As before, a combination of follow-ups and probes are quite useful:

- 'Now, how about the other side of the coin? Anything about you that you feel could be strengthened?'
- 'What are the things you feel less confident about ... things you'd like to improve?'

- 'How do you assess that? How do you gauge whether you've actually changed?'
- 'Has that had a bearing on the results you've actually achieved in your job?'

Don't end this discussion too soon. A little bit of **pressure** is quite acceptable here.

Be careful you're not getting **virtues in disguise** from the candidate. You must be wary of a person who has prepared for this and produces a few **innocuous** statements that they hope will actually cast them in a favourable light.

- 'I suppose my biggest weakness is that I expect too much from myself.'
- 'I know I get impatient with people who are content to go through the motions or who expect me to do their thinking for them.'
- 'I'm not much of a politician I suppose. I tend to call it as I see it and it's got me into hot water a few times.'

These are the sort of **self-congratulatory** comments you'd get from a sophisticated candidate. Let them talk until it's your turn and follow up with something like:

- 'Well, OK. But I can see how being too **tough** on people might also be considered a **personal strength**, depending on how you look at it. Is there anything that's really a **shortcoming** ... something that you know prevents you from achieving the sort of results that you would otherwise be capable of?'

You're letting the candidate know, without being offensive or cute, that you can **see** through their ruse. If you have to, explain again what you mean by a weakness.

4 USING A ONE-TWO COMBINATION

A good way for you to get at strengths and weaknesses is to ask the candidate to **hypothesise**:

- 'Let's imagine you've been with us for a year and you've achieved outstanding results. What are the most likely reasons for that happening?'
- 'Let's imagine that you've been here a year and we both decide that it's not working out. What are the most likely reasons for that not happening?'

5 SELF-DEVELOPMENT

Talking about the candidate's strengths and weaknesses gives you an excellent opportunity to **zero** in on their self-development. In essence, you should discuss how the candidate has fine-tuned their strengths over the years and how they've overcome their weaknesses.

- 'You've talked about your enthusiasm being a strength. Does that come naturally or is it something you've had to work at?'
- 'You've said you're interested in marketing. Have you taken any steps towards developing your career in that direction?'

6 USING A QUESTIONNAIRE

You can approach this from a different angle by giving the candidate a list of 30 relevant strengths and ask them to **earmark** their five **strongest** and the five where they are **least strong**. Follow that with the next five strongest and the next five weakest.

In effect, what you've done is ask the candidate to create their own frequency distribution that **forces** them to make choices. Then, instead of asking them to talk about their strengths and weaknesses, actually go through the results of the questionnaire together.

- 'You indicate that multi-tasking is one of your strengths. Do you think that you could expand a bit on what that term means to you?'

MAKING WHAT MATTERS WORK FOR YOU

✓ Get the candidate to talk about the specific strengths they feel have contributed to their success.

✓ Be prepared to probe for the answers you want. Don't stop until you've got them.

✓ Be wary of virtues in disguise. Make sure the candidate knows you're looking for a genuine weakness.

✓ Ask the candidate to hypothesise the future to get an insight of their strengths and weaknesses.

✓ Establish how the candidate's strengths and weaknesses have had a bearing on their self-development.

✓ Use a questionnaire to stimulate discussion with the candidate on their strengths and weaknesses.

5 Probing for Specifics

There's a lot to do during the interview. You have to guide the conversation, ask pertinent questions, make notes and keep an eye on the time.

4

things that really matter

1 EFFECTIVE LISTENING
2 THE BEHAVIOURAL DIG
3 QUESTIONS AND ANSWERS
4 PROBING FOR SPECIFICS

Up to now we've looked at how to get the candidate talking whilst avoiding question and answer sessions but now you have reached the point in the interview where questions have to be asked.

The aim of every interview is to re-create, as closely as you can, the candidate's past performance, their past behaviour, and you can only do that through the candidate's own story telling. Your only link with the past is through their own description of what happened.

There is no way of avoiding pertinent, and sometimes searching, questions at this stage if you want to ensure that what you're hearing and watching is a true reflection of events. Your task here is to penetrate the blind spots, unravel the misinterpretations, the rationalisations and the distortions to get at the facts.

Your aim is to go back in time to re-create past performance by being a fly on the wall.

IS THIS YOU?

• This candidate seems perfect for the job. Everything fits but I've got a sneaky suspicion that it's just a bit too good. I'm missing something here. • I need to find out more about the candidate's background with regard to their alleged experience in project management. • I've got two candidates who seem ideal for the job and I've now got to eliminate one of them.

EFFECTIVE LISTENING

To move the interview forward at a desirable pace you must listen effectively and this requires a lot of **mental discipline**. Here are some essential guidelines.

Make sure you're well prepared. Before the interview you should have:

- done a thorough **review** of all available information
- developed a rough **plan** for the interview and
- made sure all **documentation** is available.

Take steps to prevent interruptions. Make sure that:

- the telephone doesn't ring
- no-one knocks on the door and
- a loud discussion doesn't take place next door.

Give the candidate your full interest. You can't conduct an interview if:

- the latest sales figures are worrying
- you're concerned about a meeting later in the day or
- you're distracted by the candidate's appearance.

Do things that show you're interested. Don't just sit passively but:

- **nod** your head occasionally
- **smile** when the candidate says something humorous and
- use words and phrases to show an **interest** in what's

being said.

Use a reflective response to let the candidate know you're trying to listen and understand. You're giving them a chance to correct you if your understanding is off track.

- 'What were your reasons for leaving the company at that stage in your career?'
- 'I wasn't too happy with the way things were going and I felt a move was the best thing for both me and the company.'
- 'It sounds, then, like you and the company weren't getting on too well?'
- 'It's not so much that we weren't getting on. The problem was that I'd stopped growing in my job. There wasn't anything to look forward to and both the company and I knew it.'

By **mis-stating** what the candidate has told you you're, in effect, challenging them to give a better explanation.

Feeling the facts. The reflective response helps you to pin down the candidate's emotions and interpretations. Because feelings represent their **reactions** to facts and events they are an important source of information. For example:

- 'How did you feel about that'? or
- 'I guess that came as a bit of a blow, didn't it'?

Dealing with silence. There is always a distinct **pressure** on the candidate to say something when there is a noticeable pause in the conversation. Don't be too quick to end the silence because it's asking them what more they can add to what they've just said.

Give the process a fair chance to proceed at its own pace. A good candidate will naturally fill the time as they become more comfortable with the way you're conducting things.

Some additional guidelines. Although this is a demanding part of the process, make the interview as relaxed as you can by observing the following points:

- **Listen** for the meaning of what's been said. If you have misunderstood something, ask for clarification.
- Use **questions** to maintain **concentration**.
- Be **alert** to how things are being said. Keep a **watchful** eye on vocal mannerisms, inflection, gestures, facial expressions and body posture.
- Be as **natural** as you can.

Maintaining a positive attitude is very important. The candidate must depart feeling that they've made a positive impression.

If the candidate tells you they weren't promoted because their boss held them back, play on it. Be supportive and they will feel comfortable enough to continue in that vein. What you then hear and see is the **real candidate** coming out. More will be forthcoming if you:

- **Avoid disagreement.**
- **Use positive reinforcement.** You can create a non-judgemental climate by paying the candidate a **compliment** but make sure you're **sincere**.

2 THE BEHAVIOURAL DIG

This involves taking a **specific incident** and delving into it more deeply until you're **satisfied** with the outcome. For example:

- 'I'm still not sure why your boss stopped you going

ahead with that project. The costs weren't out of line ...

- 'I think it was more because he was apprehensive about the fall-out in Consumer Products.'
- '**What** do you mean – "fall-out"?'
- 'We'd been getting the lion's share of the funding since I took over and Consumer Products felt it was time to even up the score a bit.'
- '**Why** would that make your boss apprehensive? I'm still **not sure** about this word "fall-out"?'
- 'I think Consumer Products had put pressure on my boss for more funding.'
- 'From what you said earlier, your boss doesn't sound like the sort of person who would succumb to pressure from one of his underlings, **does he**?'

Look for discrepancies between what's being said and how it's being said and don't be afraid to point out these observations.

The behavioural dig requires you to start with a *lead-in* and then *probe, probe* and *probe* again. It should be used:

- When the candidate has reviewed their background in such **broad terms** that you haven't learned anything.
- When you sense the candidate has described things in such a way as to put themself in the most favourable light.
- When the incident being discussed is similar to those the candidate would encounter if given the job.
- When you've got first-hand experience of the situation or if it's of interest to you.

You might find that the candidate – now that they know you

won't be taken in by generalities – actually **resists** your efforts to probe for specifics. Don't react to this by over-relying on questions. Use instead one of the following:

A 'That's OK' statement. If the candidate is struggling with a silent pause to the point where it's become awkward, use something like:

- 'I know it's sometimes difficult to remember precisely what happened. It can often take a moment or two – but that's OK. We can spend a little time on this as I can learn a lot from looking at exactly what happened.'

A restatement. This requires you to make a simple restatement of the question whilst not repeating it word for word.

Polite persistence. Make sure you get evidence from your probing. The candidate must **understand** that any form of **evasion won't thwart you**.

- 'You say you're always ready to challenge the status quo. **Give** me a specific example from the past couple of months.'
- 'Well, it's something I do a lot of. It's the way I approach things. If getting on means challenging the status quo I'm not afraid to do it.'

The candidate's obviously **dodging** the question and you must make it **clear** that you will not be **satisfied** until you've got an answer.

- 'I realise it's difficult but can you give me a specific **example** of a recent situation where you challenged the status quo?'

③ QUESTIONS AND ANSWERS

If you ask the candidate a general question you're likely to get a general answer.

Generalities versus specifics. Be specific and ask the candidate exactly how they managed a project mentioned in their CV. There are three reasons for this:

- No one has probably asked them this in an interview before.
- Because of that, you'll be able to **watch** them as they actually think through the problem. It's a glorious opportunity to watch them in action.
- It comes closest to being a fly on the wall, actually watching them talk through the organisation of a project.

Behaviour versus outcomes. By digging this way you are better able to understand the candidate and predict how they will behave in the future. Let's clarify some terms:

- Behaviour is what someone actually **does**.
- Outcomes are the **result** of that behaviour.
- Environment is **where** that behaviour took place and might have **affected** its outcomes.

You need to know whether the candidate will become an outstanding performer in your environment. They will have included previous outcomes in their CV but will not have mentioned their behaviour or the environment in which it took place.

Behaviour is shaped to a significant degree by the **personality** of the individual. Therefore you can assume that certain personalities produce certain **patterns** of behaviour. You can't hire the candidate's behaviour as presented in the past but you can hire the personality that might produce it in the future.

You must re-create the environment in the interview that will, as best as you can, allow you to see the **personality at work**. If that personality becomes shifty and evasive you must question whether those same personality traits will be recognised by customers and colleagues.

4 PROBING FOR SPECIFICS

To illustrate the techniques covered in this book this section is an example of how you would question a candidate for a job as a **systems analyst**.

It's a busy, front line job with the responsibility of maintaining the computer network, developing software applications, keeping the company abreast of new technology and doing a lot of general purpose trouble shooting.

Probe for positive things first then shift your focus to the less complimentary side of the ledger.

The successful candidate will have to show an ability to handle **multiple demands** on their time and maintain a balance between long-term projects and the unanticipated daily crises that require instant attention.

It's early in the interview and you want to probe the candidate on the work they've done in this regard in the past having already started with a lead-in. So you use a follow-up:

- 'I'd like to talk a bit more about how you **organise** and **manage** your projects. Could you tell me how you do it?'

Don't be any more specific than that. When the candidate winds the conversation down you could find that they haven't covered all the points. You might see they have good planning and organisational skills but can they operate in a fast moving environment where demands hit from all sides?

Use a follow-up to the follow-up but be more **explicit**:

- 'I know in my job I have a lot of different clients to keep happy and everyone of them wants their project done yesterday. Can you think of a time when you had lots of programmes to write and little time to do them in?'

Then come the probes to flesh out the behavioural specifics.

- '**When** did this take place?'
- '**How** did you go about **allocating** your time across the different projects that had to be completed?'
- '**Did** you have to put in any overtime to get everything done?'
- '**Were** you eventually able to write all the programmes? **How** did you manage it?'
- '**How** often does this sort of logjam occur, let's say over a six-month period?'
- '**When** did this take place?' is a useful question for you to ask as it underscores your determination to probe for specifics.

Conduct the interview on two levels. To establish whether the candidate is the right person for the job you must discuss **facts** and make a **prediction**. To do so requires you to conduct the selection process on the two following levels:

- **The factual level** is where you discuss past events, experiences, decisions, thoughts, feelings, ideas, actions and reactions. This is information you acquire by digging for actual behaviour.
- **The inferential level** is where you look for the

behavioural patterns the facts contain and use them to predict future performance. By doing so you are translating facts into performance.

MAKING WHAT MATTERS WORK FOR YOU

- ✓ Make sure you're well prepared before the interview with all the information and documentation available. Take steps to prevent interruptions and give the candidate your full interest with effective listening.
- ✓ For the behavioural dig you start with a lead-in and then probe, probe and probe again.
- ✓ Look for certain patterns of behaviour and you'll find the personality you're seeking.
- ✓ Probe for the behaviour that will re-create past performance and give an insight to the future. Conduct the interview at the factual and inferential levels.

6 Making the Decision

Do we hire this person? It's time to make the big decision.

4 things that really matter

1. VISUALISING FUTURE PERFORMANCE
2. RELYING ON GUT FEEL
3. REALISING THAT NO-ONE'S PERFECT
4. RECRUITING PROACTIVELY

The interview is over. You have three other people to see or there's a meeting you should have been at five minutes ago.

There's a rule you must implement immediately. Allow at least five minutes at the end of every interview for note-taking. Make sure you record things in such a manner that you will be able to recall everything about this particular candidate after you've seen the others.

If you think it helpful, generate a checklist on the basis of the winner's profile, using your own list of criteria under each heading.

This final step of deciding whether or not to hire involves visualising the candidate in the job.

Project the candidate into situations that you can actually visualise. Jobs that you've seen handled before by others or that you've had to deal with yourself.

IS THIS YOU?

• *I've watched the candidate's behaviour during the interview process and now I'm ready to move towards making a decision.* • *I'm ready to hire the candidate and I feel excited about bringing them on board.* • *What can I do about making the hiring process easier in the future?*

1 VISUALISING FUTURE PERFORMANCE

You can now **conjure** up an image of the candidate because you've come as close as you can to re-creating their past behaviour. You've heard the **voice**, noted the **mannerisms**, seen the **actions** and **reactions** to a specific event and observed the way they dealt with a situation you presented to them. Your interviewing should leave you with an **impression** of the candidate as an outstanding performer in the job.

Making the decision should now be easy because you're no longer guessing or predicting anything. You're simply **reacting** to something you've seen.

2 RELYING ON GUT FEEL

These gut feelings are, in fact, the product of nothing more than a **definable interviewing strategy** and a teachable set of **interviewing techniques**.

Using these procedures, you'll have the ability to go beyond the simple facts of a person's background and gain insight into – or get a gut feeling for – the person themself. You can then draw meaningful **inferences** about how well they will perform in the job.

- **Trust your instincts.** You'll have probed the candidate for **specific behaviours** and then searched for

personality patterns to establish the type of person you're dealing with. If, after this, your instincts tell you to hire this candidate then do it.

- **Gauge your excitement.** You should be feeling excited about hiring this candidate. If you're **not** excited then it's a sure sign that there's **something wrong** and you must not proceed. You should hire only if you know you will have absolutely no reservations about the candidate afterwards.

3 REALISING THAT NO-ONE'S PERFECT

You must bear in mind that, no matter how much the candidate impressed you at the interview and that you have no reservations about hiring them, they will not immediately become an outstanding performer. Their introduction to your company will require some form of **management plan** and you should bear the following in mind:

- What are you going to do to identify the candidate's weaknesses?
- What type of management plan are you going to put together? Who else is going to be involved?
- How soon will you put the plan into action?

You mustn't duck these questions as this is the last part of the hiring process and you're still **investing** in your outstanding performer.

It's your responsibility to ensure that the winning candidate makes as secure and positive a start as possible. Improve their potential by **seeing** them and **talking** to them regularly. By being a **coach**. A **catalyst**. A **facilitator**.

4 RECRUITING PROACTIVELY

As a manager you can't spend too much time on the hiring process and the best way around this is to have a ready **supply** of good candidates available when you need them.

It has to be your **priority** as a manager to either keep in touch with all the outstanding performers in the industry, particularly those who are ambitiously scaling the career ladder, or get a **network** in place that will perform this task for you.

Don't leave it to chance. **Do** it.

MAKING WHAT MATTERS WORK FOR YOU

- ✓ You've observed as much as you can of the candidate and the decision should almost make itself for you.
- ✓ Recognise that gut feelings are the result of a definable interviewing strategy. Trust your instincts and gauge your excitement levels.
- ✓ Put together a management plan that will make the candidate's start with you as seamless as possible.
- ✓ Create your own recruitment agencies by keeping tabs on the outstanding performers in your industry.